NIGHT SHIFT

Poems by Karen Glenn

Raven and Crow Press, Colorado

Copyright © 2012 by Karen Glenn
Cover photo © 2012 by Karen Glenn

No part of this book may be used or reproduced in any manner without written permission except in the case of brief quotations embodied in critical articles and reviews.

For permission, contact Raven and Crow Press, 395 Boundary Lane, Carbondale, CO 81623

For Tom

Special thanks to Diane Gage and Jonathan Wells

CONTENTS

NIGHT SHIFT

Night Shift   6
Loneliness   8
The Poem Wants a Drink   9
Seduction   10
The Acrobat's Family   11
His Heart   12
Woman with Crow   14
Chimera   15
Berkeley, 1971   17
The Crossing   19
Korea   20
Night Fishing   21

CODE RED

Code Red   23
After He Lost   24
Cover Letter   25
Instructions from Collins   27
Finding Your Place in the Crowd   28
Thai Girlfriend   29
A Good Day   31
Grief   32
Dissatisfaction   33
Muslims at the Beach   34
Zoe at 15   35
Mice   36
Ellen   37
Ring   39
Cycle   40
Beatitude   41

Cherry   42
Antelope   43
At the Cannery   44
Suppose   45

CALL ME CIRCE

Call Me Circe   47
Horror Show   48
My True Story   49
Things   51
The Vampire Takes . . .   52
Wicked   53
Lost   55
Monkey Business   56
Red Riding Hood Revisited   59
Jungle Trek   60
The Seal   62
Ghosts   64

THE NAMING OF WOLVES

The Naming of Wolves   66
Autopsy   67
Note to My Mother   68
Fourteen   69
The Man in My Father's Mechanical Bed   70
In Taos   71
Treatment   72
To the Future   73
Late Afternoon   74
How to Drive in a Snowstorm   75
Moment   76
A Climber Sees a Monk   77
The Club   78

NIGHT SHIFT

Night Shift

Let us now praise the night shift—
those on the 8 to 4, the 10 to 6,

the 10-hour or 12-hour shift,
the bread bakers pounding and leavening,

the pastry cooks rolling and filling,
the sleep-deprived, the heavy-eyed,

the pale and dark ones sleeping
through their days, ambulance drivers

with their bright sirens, pilots
whose planes move like wandering stars,

the dawn-obsessed, the checkers of watches,
nurses slipping into unlit rooms,

the uniformed, the dressed-down, the truckers
with their high beams on, the wired,

the goosed up, the dragged down,
the lost and lonely selling tickets at dim windows,

girls who kick their shoes off, the ones
who walk the aisles, security staff, night watchmen,

all those who guard our nights,
unsmiling collectors of tolls, bouncers

at the after-hours bars, strummers
of guitars, ticklers of drums, working

in the shadow world where fluorescent lights
stand in for sun and flashes of neon

pass for stars. Let us praise the yawners
and those who stretch to stay awake,

coffee hounds, speed freaks, Coke drinkers,
women splashing water on their faces.

Remember the blackjack dealers with their gleaming cards,
waitresses sleepwalking from table to table,

taxi drivers with a gun in the glove,
all the weary, the fearful, the men

who never see their wives, the nervous babysitters,
those dancing to strange music, the clank

and drone of the factory machines,
printers rolling out the news,

all those dreaming of dawn and sleep
until, at last, in the first hint of light, the clerk

alone in the 7-11 counts the change in the cash drawer
and closes out the night.

Loneliness

It's fashioned of fire or charcoal.
Of course, it thrives in the dark,
but it also favors blank afternoons,
old calendars,
         the works of failed clocks.
It has a soul, a cock-eyed walk,
a special place it likes to
settle into,
         somewhere between
the socks and the boxers, the job
and the junk mail,
         the grasping heart
and the groin.

Is it distracted by money? No,
and it's not derailed by fame.
Passion is no protection:
lovers know it by five or six names.
         Experts say
you can spot it by color. One claims
it's the yellow of acid—
another, the blue
of spilled ink.

If you try to escape it, it just follows along
like a poet
         who is cobbling a language
from what's left of the human heart.

         Loneliness swears
it has something to tell you, a secret
it longs to share. It's crying out
for you on the emergency band,
scratching your name on the pawnshop door.

The Poem Wants a Drink

In the workshop, students analyze
What each poem wants, what each one
strives to be. Well, this poem is
a layabout with limited ambition. It wants
a drink.

This poem doesn't give a damn
for rhyme or reason. It only sings
off-key. It has no rhythm
in the jukebox of its soul.
It grew up without symbols.
It doesn't know from assonance.
Give it mambo lessons, and it
still won't learn to dance. It has
not one stanza with a lyric pedigree.
It's late, and getting later, and this poem
wants a drink.

Call it gray and tired. Even call it
a cliché. This poem's lived long enough
to know exactly what it means
to say: Don't be stingy
with the whiskey, baby.
                Yes, the night
has been a cruel one, and this poem
could use a drink.

Seduction

As they age, old vampires start to soften.
They seek out fewer victims. Even then, they steer
toward the sick, the dying. They oversleep—often—
delaying in their coffins well past moonrise. Here
and there, they pause to weep. They pocket
bitter souvenirs. Blood lust grows ever less hysterical,
shrinks to a flimsy craving. The oldest tourniquet
their prey, shame-faced, baste up their wounds. An oracle
once said that regret can be erotic: That's what
the graying vampire feels. Certainly, a raw priest
with a hair shirt and a rough cross, cut
into his flesh, has to be at least
as frightening as the vampire wasting on the shelf.
Tell me: Why would you fear an ancient like myself?

The Acrobat's Family

(from the painting by Picasso)

It was natural for the ape
to join them in their room.
He seemed enough like them
to be a friend.
In fact, he'd taught them quite a lot.
The ape could swing across the stage
in ways they hadn't mastered yet.
He'd learned the triple somersault much faster
than they had and could execute the trapeze catch
as well--when they were brave enough
to let him try.

It seemed too cruel to put him out at night
or cage him. He'd worked with them all day.
In the circus he wore the thick white ruff.
He looked so human then—and later
in the camp, he'd sit at Babette's feet
staring at her baby as if it were his own.
Sometimes his long fingers twitched,
and Babette, not knowing why, would hold the baby
so close that it gasped.

His Heart

My grandpa's life was lean and tough,
a streak of gristle in the teeth of God.
He was a revenuer searching

for stills in North Florida's piney woods,
a target for ticks my grandma
couldn't scrub away—no matter how hard

she boiled that water—and for tick fever
no doctor ever cured.
But God must have loved him,

God knows why, making him fall asleep
on a damp mosquito night
staked out in a Buick behind

a moonshiner's fire, slumped down
so far in that car his head
fell below the dashboard.

It was his partner, upright
in the driver's seat, who took
the bullet. Grandpa stayed slumped

on the floor, invisible 'til morning,
drove home covered in his partner's blood.
Yet it wasn't a bullet or a tick

that finally killed him, just
his own inflexible heart.
He never learned to soften;

when the pressure built, that proud heart burst.
There was not much left inside it—
a few marbles and a rubber band,

a map of the piney woods, an old photo
of my grandma with a long brown braid
she'd cut off years and years before.

Woman with Crow

    (from the painting by Picasso)

Crow, I will know you
'though you mock me—
this gaunt frame
in a pink shroud of a dress.
I am no proper woman.

When I was a child on the farm
I stood among tall stalks of corn
hiding from my sisters.
I was not one of them.
They blamed me for my unbred voice
and eyes. It was raining, and
I watched you shuddering and raw perched
on the arm of a scarecrow. In your face,
I found my own.

I have been waiting forty years to know
my hands in your damp feathers.

Chimera

This morning early, I followed
the rural roads deep into Nevada,
rolling and curving through the tiny towns
until I found the place I'd read about

where some sheep have human livers,
others human blood, and just one,
a human heart. It was in your newspaper, too,
I bet, not some H.G. Wells nightmare,

filled with beasts that groan and speak,
but a lab farm, scoured and neat,
shining with aluminum and chemicals,
a place where a liver grown

inside a sheep is not a horror, but a hope
for folks who need one. At first
it was a disappointment. In the lab and
in the field, the sheep crowded together,

baaing—looking, acting just like sheep—
nothing distinguishing about them.
But then the one with the human heart
followed the scientist who'd made him

with his eyes, watched the tracks
her small feet made across
the lab's damp floor. He stood stock still
in the stall when she touched him

with her cold instruments, then nuzzled
her soft hands. Even I could feel it.
It's something we all know—
how the heart keeps wanting, wanting

the unnameable, the impossible, yearning in the dark,
like a sheep at night in a cold barn.

Berkeley 1971

I woke this morning, remembering
a small white dog from long ago.

It was waiting in its cage at the pet store
every day when I'd go in. It stayed

locked up, while children pulled puppies
out onto linoleum, wrestled with them

on the cold and musty floor. I debated
and debated but never brought it home.

Then this evening at a party, they played
old Linda Ronstadt tunes. "I've done everything I know

to try and make you mine," one song moaned
and moaned again, 'til I broke into tears. A friend,

said it was because Ronstadt sang it
in a minor key. But I was back in Berkeley yet again.

There, in the crash pad a floor below
my room, a girl, 15, a runaway, wailed

and cried most every night. Hour after hour,
her record player blared "And I think it's gonna hurt me

for a long, long time." It groaned on well past midnight
until, near dawn, I marched downstairs.

When I found her shaking, naked, by the open window,
I backed away. Then later, feeling foolish,

I came back with hot chocolate and a blanket,
tried to tuck her into flimsy sheets. She was just bones,

not much more, on a soiled mattress on the floor.
In the small white face, the eyes focused nowhere.

The Crossing

The sky has that fishbone look tonight,
and as it darkens, two skunks begin
to cross the road. Skunks aren't fast.
They waddle, take their time to the white line,
then stroll, pigeon-toed, across
remaining blacktop, right in front
of our careening car. The sight of them
is shock enough to stop us.

Skunks get nonchalant about their enemies,
they say, a few hot sprays usually enough
to send even bobcats into awed retreat.
A speeding car could be a different thing.
But tonight, we wait and wait for them
to cross, while cars and trucks
honk just behind us, stacking up
for more than three blocks back.

The skunks look up, curious
but unconcerned about the noise.
And as we wait, the stars
slide out. Our breathing calms,
moving smoothly in and out,
out and in, growing slower,
slower in the pale evening light.

Korea

My father is sleeping in that tent again,
where every night the rats still run and run
across his body, and every night
he still slaps them—hard--away from him,
never waking, never knowing
that it's my mother's hand, soft
against his chest, reaching
for him in the dark.

Night Fishing

Lantern scans, a searchlight
over water. My father and I
are floundering. I am twelve.
He's just returned from war games
in Japan. We walk in Neuse River water,
metal gigs in hand, searching
for the tell-tale shapes of flounder.
For camouflage, they bury themselves in sand.
Still their outlines give these fish away,
like a girl's small breasts
against an outgrown sweater.

I feel lost. He's been gone two years;
he's as strange to me
as the metal poles we carry,
poles designed to stab.

The wind is hot. The stars
outline the sky in constellations.
I am afraid. I don't want to find the fish.
I would not have the heart
to lift the gig. I scuff through water,
stirring sand.

My father sees. He starts to sing.
He kicks up sand like I do.
He takes my hand. We splash, we shuffle
through the swirling water.

The fish are safe. And I am safe.
The moon shines. The lantern shines.
The water shines. My father and I
are going home.

CODE RED

Code Red

All dolled up in a ruby dress,
her fractured heart beating outside
her chest, she's a living,
breathing Frida Kahlo painting.

She slips into scarlet espadrilles
and dances a bloody tango,
her lipsticked mouth puckering as if
she's just eaten something tart.

Or wants to. Her henna hair is waving
like an SOS all over this dance hall.
God, it's flaming hot in here.
Someone call the police, the fire department!

Don't bother, she shrugs, feeling for a fever.
Just come closer. Pass me that cherry cola.
I'll be your siren, your fire alarm,
your train track beacon,
your own personal red phone.

After He Lost

two fingers in the closing door
he quit dating the senior cheerleader.
The pros wouldn't want him.
He couldn't throw a pass
with two fingers and a thumb.

It didn't hurt his lovemaking.
The girl he found was dark.
She was a poet,
he no intellectual.
They didn't waste words.
She let him know.
Those three fingers
drove her wild.

Cover Letter

Dearest Editor,
I have been a faithful and close
(very close) reader of your fine magazine
for many years. I get so excited when
I see the red flag of the mailbox
stand up and I know what's stuffed inside.
I'm positively damp palming
24-page articles on the history
of wheat and 35-page thrusts
of exegesis into the deep meaning
of the word "OK." But most of all
I love eyeing your picture
on that virginal first page. I always see
you gazing back at ME! And no matter
how my day's been, or how much
—or little—I have on, you wear
that same bittersweet, suggestive smile.

So I was bewildered when you sent back
my poem without a word, just a stark
and naked form that you didn't even take
the time to bless with ink from your thick,
trusty pen. How could you reject
my "Ruminations on a Rubber Slipped
as a Bookmark into Chapman's Homer"?
At first I was angry, but then I thought
of you. Maybe you were tense or
having a bad day. Maybe you needed
a cool hand on your forehead or a squeensy
shoulder rub.

So all is forgiven. I'm sending now
my sonnets describing each position
in the Kama Sutra, with polaroids of me

to match. I trust you'll enjoy the sketches
of my ideal partner—you!—that I etched in.
Please don't mind: I've drawn you
sans toupee (Yes, I know. Don't ask me how.)
It's because I love your round
bald head, its lubricious shine. Even
your bulging eyes, your bulbous nose,
the tips of your sharp ears hint
at so many luminous possibilities.

May I suggest that if these poems
don't satisfy, you read them
once again. I can tailor them
to meet your needs as closely
as a pair of pantyhose. Yes, I know—
don't ask me how—and I find
that little tic of yours as endearing
as I KNOW you'll find these poems.

Instructions from Collins

Once long ago, I read a poem called
"Instructions from Bly."
On his advice, a young poet went off
to taste the real world.

She ditched her MFA, hitchhiked
to North Dakota, and got a job
pumping gas out there on the plains.
Her poem had lots of dust imagery,

the smell of good clean sweat,
and the occasional diesel engine.
At times I still picture her
looking out over fields of wheat

and earning the beginnings
of a weather-beaten face.
In my workshop, Billy Collins
gives easier suggestions.

"Fix these line breaks," he opines
or "Tighten up that final stanza."
At this age, I'm grateful he doesn't say
to begin a whole new life. Still sometimes

I wish, if only for a moment
that he would tell me to quit my job
and move to a small Mediterranean island
or, perhaps, a beach house in Hawaii.

Finding Your Place in the Crowd

Just try it in this hangout, neck-deep in bimbos and flappers,
hoofers and Romeos carting drizzly ice sculptures

and insidious platters of Swedish meatballs.
It's as retro as retro gets, while you are cosmically turned out

in your state-of-the-future duds with titanium zippers
and hems that flash uranium flares. Just when you think

it's time to hit the hooch, your fairy grandmother
whirls her magic baton. Poof! You're a drum majorette

in 60's go-go boots, mini-skirt, and white-fur collar.
No need to worry—the animal rights activists all stayed
        home,

and that brylcreamed hunk in sleeveless lizardwear,
arms bright with tattooed constellations, starts sidling

for a closer look. OK, Betty, time to twirl the cat,
hoot the hoot, run the ramp, and fly! Up over

that big round object whirligigging
in the eaves like some lost moon.

No stooge you, you melt into the stars
like you belong there.

Thai Girlfriend

"Phuket is Thai girlfriend central,"
my husband says. We've seen it now
for days—middle-aged farangs

on motorbikes, Thai bar girls
perched on back. Another couple's
here tonight, sitting right behind us.

We look away, turn toward the waitress
in sailor blouse and navy skirt. Small and slender
as a schoolgirl, she's hand-decorated

her sneakers, short white socks. When we ask
about the fish, she shows us concrete basins
where grouper and white snapper swim.

She scoops them up in plastic laundry hampers.
The fish fight at first, flop themselves
onto the pavement, then give up, lie still.

After we eat, we look again at the man
and woman behind us. He's far from young,
gray hair matted in the heat.

On second glance, she's not a child either.
Her face says she's been on the back end
of the bike a few too many times.

When they get up to ride his shiny Harley,
he picks up his helmet. She'll ride without—

they always do. But, no, he stops her,
gently pushes back her hair. As she giggles
up at him, he adjusts the helmet straps
beneath her chin. And for a moment,

what looked like business
as usual seems like something more.

A Good Day

My mother was a beauty
and dressed it. One Sunday
the preacher quipped,
"Even Solomon in all his glory
was not arrayed like one of these."

Now she's 76. Thin and hairless,
she wears a cheap wig, dirty tennis shoes.
She sees poorly, drives worse.
One Monday, she hits a parked car
in the cancer patient lot. Muddled,
she just drives away. A day later,
police call. Somebody caught
her license plate number.

I'm surprised she tells this story on herself.
It's not her way. Then I hear that old tone
in her voice. The witness described me
as an attractive blond," she says,
"in her fifties."

Grief

My father set aside ten thousand dollars
for my wedding day
but reduced it by one-fourth
each year I went to college.

I not only went to college;
I earned a Ph.D.
and my father didn't live
to see me marry.

I didn't cry in the hospital room
or later at his funeral,
but I wept at a stranger's wedding
when the bride danced with her father.

Dissatisfaction

It hovers like a helicopter,
thumps like a poltergeist, creaks
like a waterlogged door. Mornings early,
it likes to lurk beneath the covers,
surprising us as we kiss, jumping out
from under the new silk sheets
like a nervous jack-in-the-box.

On rainy days, it gathers dust balls
from every corner, weaves them into a suit
for wearing everyday--and even Sundays.
Or we can find it rooting around
the refrigerator, taking the odd bite
out of the melons, rotting the vegetables,
turning the potatoes green,
the lettuce yellow.

Sometimes it even crawls right inside
our tired, fed-up bodies, hitches a ride.
Soon enough, it's pounding out
its complaints on the drums of our hearts,
making wheezy accordions out of our lungs.
Our tonsils become fiddle strings, our throats kazoos,
our intestines long, sad horns. It turns itself
into an entire makeshift blues ensemble, wailing
out its own distinctive itch and moan
like a cheap plastic radio that
just will not turn off.

Muslims at the Beach

On the ferry to Langkawi, a Malay girl in jeans
rides on deck, letting her head scarf slide

down her hair until the wind takes it.
On the island, a woman hikes up loose pants,

kick-starts a scooter, head scarf flowing out
below her helmet. In the beach cafe,

a waitress, head wrapped in white, smiles wide,
mixing mai-tais at the swim-up bar.

It's a shock to see the woman in the chador.
She's a black tent, an enormous crow,

a question mark, a Rorschach blot, a wall.
"Not from here," a Malay matron hisses.

"Maybe an Arab state." The next day its 93 degrees.
She sits in her beach chair in that chador watching

the waves. Tiny jewels frame the slit that shows
her eyes. Her husband's hand snakes along

her shoulders. What does she think of her bright sisters?
What does she think of me, crossing the strand in shorts

and T-shirt to wade in warm, shallow water? I stare at her,
and she stares back. Without a face, her dark eyes

tell me nothing. Slowly she lifts the veil that hides
her mouth, takes one small taste of orange juice.

Zoe at 15

My body swells like the water balloons
I used to throw from high up in the tree house,
It gets bigger and I get quieter,
sitting in class in my bagged-out sweater, pretending
not to know the answer to the question
growing teeth inside of me.
              To that thing, *I'm* a tree house,
a place to hide, all warm and tucked inside.
But I want to say that it's not safe,
not safe at all with me. I'm not sturdy.
I teeter on two legs more like twigs
than trees. I'm a hazard, a skate
on the stairs, an oil slick, a kite
heading for the wires.
              And to me, that thing inside
is nothing human. It's a piece of gum
I can't scrape off my shoe. Still, sometimes,
I think I feel it move. Then I put
my arms around myself. I hug myself
and it, afraid of what might break.

Mice

That summer I was young and poor and unemployed.
The man I lived with tried to love me
but somehow never managed it. I'd eavesdrop
on the other line as he set up motel sex
with women I'd had coffee with the day before.
I ignored the calls and set out poison for the mice.

The day that someone offered me a job,
I sat on the kitchen counter with the phone.
The largest mouse I'd ever seen—a rat?—
bloated, slow from poison, crawled across the floor.
I couldn't stand it. I covered it with a heavy iron pot.
It shuddered towards me, then finally stopped.

I came back that night to make sure
that it had died. Then I took the pot out
to the garbage on the stoop—bread crusts,
tissues, coffee grounds. The mouse
looked soft, a subtle shade of gray,
sleek-whiskered, smooth, clean skin.
I wasn't sure it had a soul. Still I whispered
a small prayer before I slid it in the bin.

Ellen

1. Reading the Newspaper

I unwrap fish from newspaper,
clean scales, think again
that I will cut my hair.
At night it's much too hot,
damp against John's pillow
or clinging to my neck,
a thousand tiny ropes.

I've seen this newspaper before.
*Suburban Mother Slays Husband
and Children.* She didn't give a reason.
She left the clutter of bodies across the room
like the clutter of fish entrails
and heads, the clutter of diapers
in the bathroom pail. Neighbors heard
only her sobbing, as if someone
were drowning, struggling for air.

2. Cleaning My Desk

My desk is a mountain
I can't climb. A camper
with a household on her back,
I should have stayed at home.
I don't want to look
at my unfinished drawings.
If they are windows,
they are closed. John said
*Clean up. Only keep the ones
with promise.* But they
all look alike—black lines
across white paper like barbed wire.

3. To My Child

Little mouth, you are always there.
You cling so hard I think
you *are* my breast. My milk
is not enough. You'd like to eat
me up as well.

Please go ahead. I'm here.
In a little while, you will sleep.
Little mouth, you will be quiet
for a time, until you call
me from whatever thing
I try to do. It's not a fault,
I know. Sleep, little mouth, sleep.

4. Before the Bathroom Mirror

I don't know the woman
in the mirror. When she takes
off her clothes, her skin's
too loose. It fits her body
like another dress a size
too large. It still can't cover
up the ribs; the bones
stick out like tent poles.

She's a cast-off.
She wasn't given enough hair.
She's scaly all over like a fish.
I'd like to capture all those lines
in clay, but the kitchen knives
all disappeared after I cut
my hair.

Ring

She threw her ring into the water.
A hot day, the water shimmering.
Her lover, fully dressed,
dove in to bring it back, unearthed it
from the mud at lake bottom.

A hot day. They drank champagne
on the small sailboat; music played,
a woodwind trio on the shore.
She laughed, and sunlight glimmered
as it fell through layers and
layers of water.

It seemed all bright colors and slow motion
as she put back on the wedding ring
that she'd sent flying. When she glimpsed
her lover's face, her breath caught
hard against her ribs. All around her,
birds fell through the sky—
gulls after fish.

Cycle

He meant that Harley for his death machine.
His doctor told him that
and, on the side, advised her
to sleep with him. The gospel truth,
he rode her instead of the cycle.

They first made love the day
he sold the Harley. He filled the toolbox
with pills obtained, like her,
through his psychiatrist.

But the bike had its advantages. It responded
only to his hands and not his moods.
It didn't make demands.
It never cried out in his sleep.
It was easy to maintain.

He found her lying on his bed
next to the toolbox, pills
spilled out across the floor.
That Harley was a
hoax;
she was the death cycle
who'd drag him where
he didn't want to go.

He drove her to the hospital.
He left her there.
He didn't call. He knew
she was beyond repair.

Beatitude

Blessed are the trash collectors,
for they don't ask questions.
They just put it all in the truck—
the junked jewelry, rotting rubbers,
the brushes without handles,
the blackened cassoulet.
They tell no one
about your irredeemable poetry,
torn negligees, singed feathers,
musk or melted wax.
They have their own sorrows,
no need to borrow yours. Hope hangs
like stench over your garbage, trailing
clouds of longing, the ashes
of hurt and forgiveness, the cigarette butts
of another ludicrous love. Oh, Lord,
have mercy on the garbagemen,
for they must haul it all away.

Cherry

Red car
sings out like sax
sex-hot and sweet: I'm the
best machine that ever growled down
your street.

Antelope

The old man and his wife lived alone, counting out their few remaining days. They had known each other so long that sometimes they shared the same dreams, passing them back and forth through the night like bread. This night he dreamed of antelope, his vision so intense their beauty hurt him. He lay there, crippled by his longing.

At the same time, she could feel their cool breath on her cheek. Soon she rose to join them. Her face narrowed, her sense of smell quickened, her heart beat faster. She tasted the air.

That morning he woke to find her gone. When he looked out the bedroom window, he saw a herd of antelope leaping in their small back yard. Flying through the air, they hung suspended for a moment, framed by the trees and the sky.

At the Cannery

I never thought of your clubfoot.
We worked the night shift,
watched those tomato cans come
sliding down that conveyor belt
as easily as your hard prick slid into me
when we made love behind the packing boxes.
Drugs and summer heat softened those long nights,
warmed them into a blur of dust and lovemaking
almost untouched by that constant whir
of necessary machinery.

When canning season ended, I walked out
into that too bright morning,
shook off your limp,
hitched back to school.

Suppose

everything is okay. There really is
nothing to worry about. Days go by,
a trainload of marshmallows.
You have no problems;
the sky is clear as vodka.
The rain doesn't fall, but the oleanders,
the magnolias, the insistent camellias
keep right on blooming.
                Winter is banished.
Spring starts over again,
pushing its way out of the earth,
each and every dawn, like a beautiful corpse
that really can rise again.
                Your lover is faithful now,
brings champagne every afternoon.
Each evening, under the unchanging stars,
the sex is so good that, even when you try,
you can't stop coming.
                There is no death,
no aging. You stay just as you are.
And if anything bothers you,
it is only the slightest twinge.
You can't even feel it, as you stare out
across that ever-blue horizon, where the future
goes on and on and on, looking
exactly like today.

CALL ME CIRCE

Call Me Circe

They say I like to turn men
into swine. It's not the truth.
I just can't help it.
I bite my lip. I swing my hip.
There are a thousand tricks,
each one of them too easy.
It's no work for a woman.
A prepubescent girl could do it.
The proof? That Daphne, a disaster really
with her bared baby breasts.
But spying her, sun-dazed Apollo
became a goat in rut. To get away,
she had to turn into a tree—
a laurel, I believe.

A laurel! A pretty tree,
but pointless. That wouldn't be my way.
No, picture this—that green tree
swaying back in Eden, a snake
curled in the branches. That's more me.
My treacherous apples hang
not quite out of reach, promising
everything,
         everything
like some deceitful god.

Horror Show

Spiders hang
suspended
in mid-air.
The faucet doesn't
drip. The razor
doesn't rust.
Even the dust
collects
too slowly.

For years there's been
no sign of the monster.
The dog bites
its tongue
to keep from
barking.
The scientist prepares
peas and mashed potatoes.
The woman is tired
of searching for footprints.
The man sits cleaning
a revolver.

My True Story

I started out a woman
so gorgeous even goddesses
smashed their mirrors in despair.
No wonder that Poseidon
wanted me . . . but my bad luck.
Could I say no?
              He was a god!
I don't regret the hours we spent
on passion's roiling seas
except the last, there in Athena's temple.

When that jealous virgin found us
naked, perfect bodies coupled there
inside her lonely shrine, she punished
only me. Poseidon slunk back home
to dried out Amphitrite. But I was made a gorgon,
bedecked with claws, festooned with serpents
like ribbons in my hair.

Despite it all, men *still* could glimpse
the girl I used to be. That shadow stopped them
like a ghost. They stood around like ice sculptures,
flash-frozen for eternity.

I was sole curator of this sad display;
only I could stop it. So when Perseus came
for me, I bowed to his advance. Then
from my spilled blood
                sprang Pegasus. Now I know
what beauty is—not some plumped up pair
of lips or breasts, caught for a moment

in a mirror or a sea god's wandering eye.
No, it's stout legs, a fearless heart
and wings, beating strong
and unrepentant against the smug,
reproachful sky.

Things

           turn in on themselves
like the eyes of a ghost.
Nothing is like they told you.
Listen.
        Inside this shell
a monsoon is raging.
At the center of the storm
a tiger's single footfall
on the grass.

The Vampire Takes His Girlfriend's Family to Dinner

It's the best place in town,
and Vlad wears black, of course,
to match his lank, black hair.
A diamond stud shines in each ear;
his face is night-light white.
His girlfriend Vi is black-haired, too.
Her sister Sal is all confused.
Vi used to be a blond like her. Sal smooths
her shell-pink shirt, her paisley skirt.
She blinks at Vlad. Is he a rock star?
She hasn't heard a word
about how and where they met.

The parents are wondering just where
they went wrong. First Vi saw that biker,
then a poet, then a juggler, then a mime.
They watch in shock as Vlad and veggie Vi
finish off some bloody steaks.
Still Dad trots out a smile when Vlad
retrieves the check. Tentative, Vi's mom
leans in to kiss him on the cheek.
Unlike the last one, this guy talks
although he looks a bit too old for Vi.
Oh, what the hell, Mom thinks. So what
if his teeth are just a little long!
At least he has some cash.
Maybe Vi *should* go with him
to Transylvania (wherever that is). The girl's
not getting younger after all.

Wicked

First my mother died. Then my father
found himself a whore who wouldn't love me
'though I plucked eyes from potatoes,
strung beans, raked coals,
filed her scowling daughters' nails.
Even then I sensed magic, the file
shivering and pulsing in my hand.

My powers scared me. So I ran away,
the streak of evil in me small then,
barely a crack, a vein no bigger
than your own. And one night, late,
I made love to a young prince.
"Cinderella," he whispered.
So I answered him.

The wedding over, his caresses stopped.
He started slipping off to other fairy tales.
There was a pale, dark-haired girl. A dwarf cult
displayed her in a clear glass case. He saved her
when he tongued away a piece
of poison apple in her mouth. Next?
He climbed a rope of hair, just to stroke
a breast, a body in a tower.

When we were alone,
he had a fetish, trying to stuff
my feet into smaller
and smaller
shoes.   When they wouldn't fit,
what could I do? Feet bleeding,
I stumbled out into the dark
where the wildness in me hardened,

then shattered like ice. Evil surged
through me, like damp
through a sponge.

Those who hurt me fear me now.
With one quick blink
I've turned some into worms
or pond scum. Don't act surprised.
Where did you think
that witches came from?

Lost

Hansel and Gretel, betrayed by birds,
their trail markers eaten, made it home

at last, their faces smeared with cake,
the witch's hallucinogenic icing.

Still no one believed their story.
Even their glad father figured

they were overdramatizing.
Later on, they wondered

if it was then they lost their way.
Should they have stayed

in the dark gingerbread forest forever
instead of coming home to homework,

school, chores and chopping wood?
So soon they lost their sense of fear

and wonder, thrill and sway;
so quickly, they slipped back

into the throb and squabble
of the everyday.

Monkey Business

THUNDER?   Someone
breaking in?

No!
The give-away's
the

t
a
i
l

hanging
in
the
upstairs
window.

Langurs are foraging
on the roof,   throwing
                            half-eaten fruit

to the ground
like rejected ideas.

Bang!

Bang!

They   leap   from
                          branch   to   branch

from tree
                        to tree,

suspended
                        in the air like
                                        stretched-out
question marks.

Tree limbs

d
e
s
c
e
n
d

bounce,
back again
                    tremble,   bounce

How long
        can branches
                      hold before

limbs   and   langurs   both

come
crashing
down?

They keep   leaping
                                          like
                                  grasshoppers,

   like flying squirrels,

   like

            they've just invented

                        free association.

Red Riding Hood Revisited

The forest was as lush as magic, and
Red Riding Hood was old enough
to know better. But when the wolf
moved close to her, she knew only
that his eyes were yellow, and
he smelled like trees. The picnic basket
opened. The found chocolate mousse and wine.
Her head bobbed lower and nearer and
finally touched his shoulder. He felt
as happy as if he'd eaten a drugstore.

As for the rumors, the neighbors
were wrong. The wolf never even touched
her grandmother. He and Red Riding Hood
fell in love. Together they grew
as fat as stones, drinking whiskey and water,
and rolling into nights as sweet and ripe
as pears.

Jungle Trek

We follow our Malaysian guide—
we call him Uncle Yip—into the woods,

climbing steps hewn from roots of trees.
("It's like Swiss Family Robinson,"

one woman chirps.) And it's all safe.
The monitor lizard, six feet long,

sporting a wicked tail, lies
on river rock, completely

out of range. For all we know
a motor flicks that tail around.

The pit viper has been asleep
for 40 days and nights, digesting

his last meal. Bats hang in palms,
and hornbills look down

on us, much more tame
than the peacocks who squawk

through breakfast every morning.
(No one believes Yip when he says

a python ate one of them a few weeks back.)
At trek's end, a man reaches out to give

a macaque monkey a peanut.
It hisses at him, backing up a tree.

When he tries again, the monkey opens
its mouth wide. And as the man begins

to yelp in pain, we see the monkey's teeth,
at least, are genuine.

The Seal

1. Seal Dreams

A seal is crippled on the land.
The woman must carry her many days
to return her to the sea.
Without the sea, the seal will die.
Sometimes as she stumbles in the snow,
the woman fears the seal has died,
or will die, or she herself will die
before the cold will end.

Sometimes the dreamer is the woman,
sometimes the seal.

2. An Irish Legend

Seals were once women
who offended gods.
Yet if a seal saves a human life,
she can become a woman once again.
Then she is more damned than before.

On nights when the moon is full,
her dark eyes will not close.
She moves in fits
as the sea sounds in her ears
and she can not escape
her human skin.

3. Song

Still in winter
I stand among the rocks

watching the seals.
I am silent through the moonlit night
awaiting their approach.

They will stare into my eyes.
Each of us will know the other.
The seals' eyes will be brown
and almost human. Mine
will reflect the cold, blank face
of the sea.

Ghosts

The ghost of Christmas future, the ghost
of Christmas past. The ghost
of Hamlet's father, the ghost
of Poe's Lenore. The ghost
caught in a tree of burning fireflies. The ghost
with eyes of coal.

The ghost with missing fingers.
The ghost who knows your name.
Ghosts swaying, drunk on memory.
The ghost of winter, settling
on you slowly. The ghost
of love, the ghost of loveliness.
That ghost, your heart, invisible as absence,
sad as hope.

THE NAMING OF WOLVES

The Naming of Wolves

The fat wolf, the thin wolf, the wolf
in old-fashioned dress and high collar.

The pale wolf, the drugstore wolf,
the wolf reading over my shoulder.

The wolf in the firelight. The wolf
of desire. The wolf of hunger, ripe

for a kill. The wolf with stones
in its belly. The wolf of fear,

gliding like water. The wolf
of loneliness. Its yellow eyes.

The wolf at the end of the story.

Autopsy

A bird falls out of the sky,
collides with New York pavement.
"Dead. Already dead," a young woman tells me.
"A woodpecker, maybe."

The woman—freckled, slim—reminds me
of the nurse my mother had last year,
there at the end. She reaches into her purse,
pulls out a pair of tweezers. "The bird –
there's something in its mouth.
It must have choked to death."
She tugs on what might be a worm.

"Do you know about birds?" I ask.
She nods, then says, "That thing
in its mouth? It's just its tongue."

She turns to catch a bus. Alone,
I study the soft, feathered body,
brown with black stripes, white petticoats,
its head with a tuft of red,
wings still stippled yellow.
It's a dead bird, I tell myself.
That's all. I don't know why
I want to push that tongue
back in its mouth
before I go.

Note to My Mother

I sit down with pen and paper,
and suddenly you're there beside me.
"Real poets," you announce,
"write about their mothers." I nod
but don't look up. It's pointless.
"Not ready yet," I mumble.
I hold my pen so tight it hurts.

The only sound from you: a snort,
then the click of heels.
You're wandering out into the yard, cutting
the camellias. I hear the snap
of scissors, the snap of stems.
The too sweet smell of flowers,
their little deaths, drifts in.

I listen hard, but now you're gone again.
You never stay. You're not some ghost
who haunts, or bares her face.
It's always only flashes of sound,
raw feeling, that spark, then burst. Mother,
what am I supposed to do? What can I do
with *this?*

Fourteen

The crabbing docks seemed innocent by day
although they faced the graveyard.
Girls ran past headstones and pulled in fish
and crab for family dinner.

Moonlight changed them. At midnight,
empty beds appeared all over town.
Mothers grew hysterical, imagining daughters
out of doors and into young men's arms,
while the girls stood silent in the graveyard
daring each other but afraid to touch the stones,
suddenly luminous as if a lantern
lit them from the dock.

The Man in My Father's Mechanical Bed

1. Outside intensive care, a sign indicates that visitors are allowed for ten minutes each hour. At the top of the hour, I'm not sure I recognize the man in my father's mechanical bed.

2. He tries to speak, but tubes down his throat and up his nose make words hard to decipher.

3. The necessary machinery blinks and clicks.

4. The smell of urine mingles with that of antiseptic.

5. A nurse in gray taps a watch, signaling me to go. A mouth opens but no words come out.

6. On the TV blaring in the waiting room, Ali McGraw has not stopped wasting away.

7. In less than 10 minutes, I've forgotten the name of her disease and its prognosis.

8. When a name squawks and crackles over a loudspeaker, it is mine.

9. Afterwards, I stand in the fluorescent glow of a vending machine stocked with Snickers bars.

10. My quarters are cold in my pocket.

In Taos

Old women sell icons, milagros,
medals of the saints, bleached white bones.
The wind topples the wooden crosses,
scatters their flowers and ribbons.
Can there be so many dead?
The sagebrush hides its deep, strange smell.
Miles of split-rail fences bend the horizon.
God has a darker skin.

Treatment

In a Chinese restaurant, a woman sits alone,
bright jacket hanging off her chair
like a red flag. Across the room,
young suckling pig hangs
behind a counter, naked, pink,
like her bare scalp.
                      Next to her,
a man gets a fortune cookie. He picks it up,
reconsiders, puts it down. On the other side,
a blond, hair trailing to her waist,
keeps her leather jacket on and reads romance.
The waiter sags against a chairback,
staring out at snarled traffic.

All around, steam rises
like smoke from an ashtray.
It is cloudy indoors and out.

The man eats his cookie, leaves
his fortune on his plate. When he's gone,
the woman bends to read it. But the waiter zooms in,
scoops the dish away. The room flutters as noodles wiggle
upward into sucking mouths.

The woman's cookie comes. She can barely breathe:
"You are about to hear an important announcement."

Sun crashes through the plate-glass window.
The blond repairs her lipstick
in a little mirror.

To the Future

There you go again, changing
lost beagles into D.E.A. agents,
nightingales into fire alarms.
What barrel are you throwing
us over this time? The sound
of your shadow stalks us. Any second
you'll up-end the sidewalk and send us
staggering into the deer-proof electric fence.

We're getting a little old for this, looking
for a stair rail, a husband's face,
an address book, a worn sneaker
to hang on to. But you're busy rewriting
the dress code. What is it this time?
Flight suits or padded bras?
Army green or cool melon?

I want a break. Slow down this convoy
for a while. Let's try to get a bead
on that bright streak firing up
the horizon. It's a little teaser,
the lead light in an exploding galaxy,
in a universe breaking apart even faster
than our own jerry-rigged hearts.

Late Afternoon

The blackberry climbs
the hard dry cliff, stretching
toward the clouds, as if
to draw the rain from them.
Where has the day gone?
My dead mother's voice
whirs, a wasp in my ear.

How to Drive in a Snowstorm

1. Turn on the car engine.

2. Get out of the car. Scrape off the snow and ice.

3. Get back in the driver's seat. Start driving. Notice the feel of the wheels as they roll.

4. Drive a little slower.

5. Watch the snow blowing across the road. Turn on the wipers.

6. Drive a little slower.

7. See the stranded cars and trucks.

8. Drive a little slower.

9. Strain to see out the front window.

10. Try the brakes. Notice how you slide sideways.

11. Turn off the engine.

12. Get out of the car. Stand in the snow. Close your eyes. Feel the snow in your face. Let it wake you. Open your mouth wide and taste the snow. Remember your childhood. Listen as the flakes fall, the slight ping of ice crystals against metal and glass. Smell winter all around you, cool as steel. Open your eyes. Notice the snow on your lashes. Look up at the strange patterns in the clouds. What do they mean?

13. Breathe deeply. Wait for the mountains to emerge from behind the curtain.

Moment

Two mule deer stand in a meadow, all brush
and flowers. One, a few feet in front,
stares straight at the camera, his eyes
dark, the lashes so thick that you know

they will show in the photo. His antlers
are soft brown, still covered with the skin
that they call velvet, his ears wide
with listening. The other's glance

is sidelong, as if he won't admit you are there.
The prairie grass around them seems to burn
in this light. The flowers --purple asters
and larkspur, monkshood and fireweed--move

and sway in the wind, just as they would
if you had never been born.

A Climber Sees a Monk on the Trail

If the body's a temple   then climbing
is praying. There's a prayer   in the timing

boot taps on the trail.   There's a note   a throb
sensed in one step   the next   felt in timing

of heartbeat   of pulse beat   the rising pump
of each breath.   What's the body's own timing?

Its hum birth to death?   What's the body's rough
clock-tick   its engine   its psalm?   The timing

is rhythm   sweet bebop for God.   Listen.
You hear it?   The body's praise song?   *Climbing.*

The Club

On the library bulletin board
I see a notice for a club
on facing death. It isn't for the dying
but a goad to the well
"to be actively alive as if
this year could be your last."

Ten years ago, the doctor said,
"Karen, I won't let you die."
Until her words, I'd never thought
it was a possibility. They talk
about "survivors" being brave.
I wasn't. I sleepwalked through it all—
chemo, cutting, throwing up, lost breast,
bald head.

My friend Kathy said that in her cancer year,
red was redder, breezes sweeter.
But when it was finally over,
she was glad not to have to appreciate
each and every damned flower.
Afterwards, she said, it brought her joy
to stand and curse a subway train
that passed us by.

Acknowledgments

Some poems in this volume, some in slightly different form, originally appeared in the following magazines:

Atlanta Review: The Vampire Takes His Girlfriend's Family to Dinner
Blue Sofa Review: My True Story
Café Solo: Cycle
Chariton Review: Finding Your Place in the Crowd, Ring
Chattahoochee Review: Note to My Mother, The Poem Wants a Drink
Contact II: Horror Show
Cream City Review: Call Me Circe
Denver Quarterly: At the Cannery
Ekphrasis: Woman with Crow
Greater Golden Hills Poetry Express: After He Lost
Greenfield Review: The Seal
GSU Review: Treatment
Hawaii Review: Beatitude
Hiram Poetry Review: The Naming of Wolves
Laurel Review: Loneliness
Lullwater Review: Korea
National Forum: Seduction
New Millennium Writings: The Club
Nimrod: Antelope, To the Future, Wicked
North American Review: Chimera, Cover Letter, Muslims at the Beach, Night Shift
Poetry Northwest: Night Fishing
Portland Review: A Good Day, Dissatisfaction, Zoe at 15
Red Rock Review: Ellen
River Oak Review: Autopsy
Seattle Review: Suppose
Southern Humanities Review: Cherry
Water-Stone: A Climber Sees a Monk on the Trail

Anthologies

The Third Rail: *The Poetry of Rock and Roll* (MTV Books, Pocket Books), Edited by Jonathan Wells: Berkeley, 1971

The Night Shift (Fives Leaves Publications, UK) Edited by Michael Baron, Andy Croft. And Jenny Swanson: Night Shift

"Night Shift" (the poem) was also broadcast on National Public Radio's *All Things Considered*. You can listen to it at www.npr.org/templates/story/story.php?storyId=1263716

About the Author

Karen Glenn's poems have appeared in *Poetry Northwest, Cream City Review, Nimrod, Seattle Review, Southern Humanities Review, National Forum, Water-Stone, Chattahoochee Review, Cricket,* and many others. *North American Review* nominated her for a Pushcart Prize. She has been a finalist in the Four Ways Books poetry book contest and the Center for Book Arts poetry chapbook contest. She has read her poetry on NPR's *All Things Considered.* She has studied with Billy Collins, Christopher Merrill, Dorianne Laux, Tony Hoagland, Jane Hirshfield, and others. She works as a writer and photographer in Colorado.

www.ingramcontent.com/pod-product-compliance
Lightning Source LLC
Chambersburg PA
CBHW060851050426
42453CB00008B/939